ANCIENT CIVILIZATIONS

ANCIENT ROME

JANE BINGHAM

WORLD ALMANAC® LIBRARY

Please visit our web site at: www.worldalmanaclibrary.com
For a free color catalog describing World Almanac® Library's list of high-quality books
and multimedia programs, call 1-800-848-2928 (USA) or 1-800-387-3178 (Canada).
World Almanac® Library's fax: (414) 332-3567.

Library of Congress Cataloging-in-Publication Data

Bingham, Jane.
    Ancient Rome / by Jane Bingham.
        p. cm. — (Ancient civilizations)
    Includes bibliographical references and index.
    ISBN 0-8368-6191-4 (lib. bdg.)
    1. Rome—Civilization—Juvenile literature.   I. Title.
    DG78.B56   2006
    937—dc22   2005051694

This North American edition first published in 2006 by
World Almanac® Library
A Member of the WRC Media Family of Companies
330 West Olive Street, Suite 100
Milwaukee, WI 53212 USA

Project editor: Kirsty Hamilton
Designer: Simon Borrough
Maps: Peter Bull
World Almanac® Library editor: Gini Holland
World Almanac® Library art direction: Tammy West
World Almanac® Library cover design: Dave Kowalski
World Almanac® Library production: Jessica Morris

Picture credits: Jonathan Blair / Corbis: Title page, pp. 3, 9; ML Sinbaldi / Corbis: p. 4;
Adam Woolfitt / Corbis: p. 6; Jeffrey L. Rotman / Corbis: p. 7; akg-images: p. 8; Bettmann
/ Corbis: pp. 10, 43; Araldo de Luca / Corbis: pp. 11, 22, 26, 27, 31, 37; Charles and Josette
Lenars / Corbis: pp. 12, 14, 41; Vittoriano Rastelli / Corbis: p. 13; Homer Sykes / Corbis:
p. 15; Seamus Culligan / ZUMA / Corbis: p. 16; Mimmo Jodice / Corbis: pp. 17, 32, 38, 39;
James L. Amos / Corbis: p. 18; Dave Bartruff / Corbis: p. 19; Roger Wood / Corbis: pp. 20,
25; Macduff Everton / Corbis: pp. 21, 34; akg-images / Erich Lessing: pp. 23, 33; Eriol Ciol
/ Corbis: p. 24; Archivo Iconografico, S.A. / Corbis: p. 28; akg-images / Robert O'Dea: p. 29;
Richard Hamilton Smith / Corbis: p. 30; Sandro Vannini / Corbis: p. 35; Gustavo Tomsich
/ Corbis: p. 36; CRDPHOTO / Corbis: p. 40; Christie's Images / Corbis: p. 42; John & Dallas
Heaton / Corbis: pp. 44, 45.

Printed in China

1 2 3 4 5 6 7 8 9 10 09 08 07 06

CONTENTS

WHO WERE THE ROMANS?

T he first Romans were farmers and hunters who belonged to a tribe called the Latins. Around 750 B.C., the Latins began to settle on the banks of the River Tiber, in the land that is now Italy.

Gradually, this settlement grew into the city of Rome, and the Latins became known as Romans.

ETRUSCANS AND GREEKS

The Romans were strongly influenced by two older civilizations: the Etruscans and the ancient Greeks. The Etruscans lived in northern Italy and were great traders, architects, and engineers. They passed on their knowledge of these subjects to the Romans, who also copied the Etruscan customs of holding chariot races and gladiator fights.

The land to the south of Rome was dominated by the Greeks who had formed colonies there. The Greeks had

Rome's ancient city center: the Forum Romanum

What does it tell us?

The Forum Romanum (*shown here*) was the grandest of all the public squares in Rome. Its oldest buildings date from around 500 B.C., and by the time of the Roman Empire, it was filled with impressive government buildings, temples, and shops. Even though these structures are now in ruins, they still give an idea of the power and glory of ancient Rome.

▲ This map shows the Roman Empire at its largest, under the Emperor Hadrian in A.D. 117.

established a magnificent civilization based around the city of Athens, which flourished from the eighth to the third century B.C. By 140 B.C., however, Greece had become part of the Roman world. Roman art, architecture, and religion were all strongly influenced by the ancient Greeks, while Roman thinkers and scientists copied many of the Greeks' philosophical and scientific ideas.

THE RISE OF THE ROMANS

By the third century B.C., Rome was a wealthy city, but it was surrounded by enemy tribes. Gradually, the Romans conquered all their enemies and gained control of Italy. Then they fought wars to win land in northern Africa and what is now called Spain. By the year 27 B.C., when Augustus became the first Emperor of Rome, the Romans controlled most of the area around the Mediterranean Sea. Over the next 150 years, the Romans created a vast and powerful empire.

The Roman Empire reached its largest size in A.D. 117, under the emperor Hadrian. At that time, the Empire stretched from Britain in the north—where London was first established as a Roman city—to northern Africa in the south, and reached as far east as present-day Iraq.

ROMAN CITIES

Wherever the Romans conquered, they set up towns and cities that were modeled on Rome, and introduced the Roman way of life. Each area (or province) of the Empire was ruled by a governor, while members of the Roman army kept the peace. The governors made sure that all the people in their provinces paid their taxes, obeyed the Roman laws, and respected the Roman gods.

All over the Empire, the Romans built well-planned cities and towns. Each town had its own public buildings and temples, as well as houses, shops, and snack stalls. Most towns had a set of public baths, and the larger cities had a theater and an arena (for shows and races). Roman towns had fresh running water in their fountains and baths, and a system of underground sewers.

A provincial city: ruins of Arausio

What do they tell us?

A triumphal arch and a theater survive from the Roman city of Arausio, (now the city of Orange, in southern France). The remains of these grand buildings (*as seen below*) show that the Romans built great cities in the provinces, and did not concentrate all their efforts just on Rome.

TRADE AND TRADERS

Trade was very important in the Roman Empire, and goods of all kinds were brought into Rome. The most important trading goods were grain, olive oil, and wine, but the Empire also imported more exotic items, such as spices from the East, silk from China, and ivory from Africa. Every part of the Empire was linked to Rome by road, river, or sea, and some adventurous Roman merchants reached as far as Scandinavia and Russia.

DECLINE AND FALL

By the fourth century A.D., the Roman Empire was weakening. Meanwhile, warlike tribes from the north were launching savage attacks on the Roman provinces. In 395, the Empire split permanently into two. The western half was ruled from Rome, and the eastern half had its own capital in Constantinople, present-day Istanbul, Turkey. The western Empire came to an end in 476, when the city of Rome was invaded by a tribe of Visigoths. The eastern Empire lasted for another thousand years. As the memory of the Roman Empire faded, the eastern half became known as the Byzantine Empire.

HOW WERE THE ROMANS RULED ?

Early Rome was ruled by kings. The king was chosen by a group of elders who also formed a council to advise the king. No accurate records exist for this period, but, according to Roman legend, there were seven kings of Rome, and the last three were Etruscans.

Under the Etruscan kings, Rome became a powerful, well-run city. The Roman people, however, hated being ruled by the Etruscans, and the last king was the most unpopular of all. Known as Tarquinus Superbus (Tarquin the Proud), he ruled without consulting the council and put to death anyone he pleased. The Roman people decided to drive Tarquin out of the city and did so in about the year 510 B.C. They swore they would never be ruled by a king again.

Tarquin's story: Livy's History of Rome

What does it tell us?

We know the story of Tarquin through the writings of Livy. He was a historian (*shown here*), who lived five hundred years after Tarquin ruled. Livy's massive *History of Rome* was based partly on folktales handed down by generations of Romans. His account is full of dramatic scenes, such as Tarquin hurling the previous king down the council steps to his death.

What does it tell us?

The initials SPQR were carved on buildings and statues during the Roman Republic, and the same letters can still be seen in the streets of Rome today. SPQR stands for "Senatus Populusque Romanus," which is Latin for "The Senate and the people of Rome." These initials reminded people that the city belonged not only to the senate but also to all the Roman people.

During the Republic, Rome was ruled by a group of powerful senators who were elected by the Roman people. This sculpture shows the head of a Roman senator. ▼

THE ROMAN REPUBLIC

After the Roman people had banished Tarquin, they set up the Roman Republic, which lasted for almost five hundred years. The Republic was ruled by the senate, a group of powerful men (called senators) who came from Rome's most important families. Within the senate, two leaders—known as consuls—were chosen each year to rule Rome .

Most Romans believed it was much better to be ruled by a senate than by a king. Even so, not everyone was happy. The ordinary Roman people—known as the plebeians—wanted more power. Some plebeians led riots against the senate and even threatened to set up a city of their own. In 366 B.C., a Plebeian Council was established to represent the views of the ordinary people. After 287 B.C., all decisions of the Plebeian Council had to become law—even if the senate didn't agree.

THE END OF THE REPUBLIC

By the second century B.C., the Roman Republic was facing problems. The Roman lands were growing fast and becoming hard to control. Meanwhile, powerful army generals were hungry for more power—and the most ambitious of all was Julius Caesar.

In 49 B.C., Julius Caesar marched with his army to Rome and seized power. He made good laws to help the poor, but, in 44 B.C., he declared himself ruler for life. A group of Roman senators feared that Caesar was becoming much too powerful, so they created a plot to kill him.

▲ Julius Caesar was an excellent general and leader of men. He is shown here leading the Roman army.

The Death of Caesar: Plutarch's account

What does it tell us?

Julius Caesar had a very dramatic death. He was stabbed to death in the senate house by the men who used to be his friends. We know the details of his death because of a lively account by the historian Plutarch (A.D. 46–126). In the sixteenth century, the English playwright William Shakespeare adapted Plutarch's *Life of Caesar* and turned it into a famous play, *Julius Caesar*. Plutarch wrote:

"…those who had prepared themselves for the murder bared each of them his dagger, and Caesar, hemmed in on all sides, whichever way he turned confronting blows of weapons aimed at his face and eyes, driven hither and thither like a wild beast, was entangled in the hands of all; for all had to take part in the sacrifice and taste of the slaughter. And the pedestal was drenched with his blood, so that one might have thought that Pompey himself was presiding over this vengeance upon his enemy, who now lay prostrate at his feet, quivering from a multitude of wounds. For it is said that he received twenty-three; and many of the conspirators were wounded by one another, as they struggled to plant all those blows in one body."

GREAT EMPERORS

A period of conflict followed Caesar's death and, in 27 B.C., the democratic Roman Republic came to an end: Augustus was made the first Emperor of Rome. Augustus was a strong and efficient ruler and a great army general. After the death of Augustus, over one hundred emperors ruled, from A.D. 14 to A.D. 476.

Some of the Roman emperors were outstanding leaders. In the first century A.D., Titus and Trajan led the Roman army in great conquests. Marcus Aurelius, who ruled in the second century A.D., was a talented commander and a philosopher, while, in the fourth century, the Emperor Constantine, the first Christian emperor, reunited a divided Roman Empire and allowed Christians to worship freely.

MAD, BAD, AND DANGEROUS

Sadly, not all the Roman emperors were great men—and some were truly terrible. For example, Tiberius, who became Emperor after Augustus, had all his enemies put to death, while the next emperor, Caligula, may have been insane. Nero, who ruled from A.D. 54 to 68, had his wife and mother murdered. In the second century A.D., the Emperor Commodus wasted vast amounts of public money on gory gladiator fights and races.

This statue shows the Emperor Augustus in military dress. By the time of his death in A.D. 41, most people had accepted the idea of being ruled by an emperor. ▶

Twelve Caesars remembered: the stories of Suetonius

What do they tell us?

The Roman historian Suetonius (A.D. 69–140) produced a series of lively portraits of the first twelve Roman caesars, or emperors, describing their achievements and their weaknesses. In his biography of Caligula, he depicts the emperor as a crazed monster who once ordered his soldiers to attack the sea. Suetonius's *Lives* were often amusing, but they also had a serious purpose. They revealed that great power could sometimes fall into dangerous hands.

HOW DID THE ROMANS EXTEND THEIR RULE?

The Romans used their highly efficient army to win lands far away from Rome. Once they had conquered an area, soldiers built strong forts to defend their position. The army also built excellent roads to connect their newly won lands to the rest of the Roman Empire.

CENTURIES, COHORTS, AND LEGIONS

By the time of the Empire, the Roman army was extremely well-organized and its soldiers fought in highly disciplined groups. The smallest unit was the *contuberium*—a group of eight soldiers who lived and fought together. Ten *contuberia* made up a century (80 men), and six centuries made a cohort (480 men). The largest unit was the legion, which was made up of ten cohorts.

Altogether, the Roman army had a total of 25 to 35 legions, but this number varied at different times of the Empire. As well as soldiers, each legion also included messengers, builders, engineers, and doctors. Together, these members of the Roman army conquered all the lands around the Mediterranean and beyond.

◀ Roman legionnaires wore metal helmets and breastplates to protect their heads and upper bodies (like the ones in this modern Roman battle reenactment). They also wore leather sandals studded with nails to give the shoes a better grip.

A military record: Caesar's *The Gallic Wars*

What does it tell us?

Julius Caesar (100-44 B.C.) was a great military leader who led campaigns in Spain and Gaul (present-day France) and even reached as far as Britain. He wrote detailed accounts of his military campaigns in seven volumes, called *The Gallic Wars*. Caesar's accounts provide valuable information about how his men were organized.

TYPES OF SOLDIERS

The Roman Imperial army contained several types of soldiers. Foot soldiers, known as legionnaires, fought with swords and javelins (long spears). They wore metal helmets and breastplates and carried large wooden shields to defend themselves. Cavalry soldiers used the same weapons but fought on horseback.

Centurions were each in charge of their own century and led their men into battle wearing a distinctive helmet with a scarlet horsehair plume. Legates commanded the legions, while generals took charge of a whole army. Legates and generals wore splendid golden helmets crowned with special crests.

In addition to the fighting men, there were also standard bearers, who carried their legion's emblem, and horn-blowers, who sent signals to the soldiers in battle. These important figures often wore the skin of a lion or a bear.

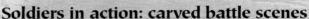

Soldiers in action: carved battle scenes

What do they tell us?

After winning a battle, the Romans often built a victory column or a triumphal arch to remind people of their great victory. These grand structures were covered with carvings showing scenes from the battle. One of the most famous victory monuments is Trajan's Column in Rome (*shown here*). It was built around 100 A.D. by the emperor Trajan to celebrate and record his victory over Dacia in Eastern Europe.

ARMS AND ARMOR

The Romans did not fight just with swords and spears. They also had an impressive range of equipment to help them attack an enemy city. Soldiers used huge wooden catapults to hurl heavy stones at their enemies. They smashed down gates and walls with battering rams on wheels. Roman carpenters built tall wooden siege towers that could be rolled up close to a city's walls. Soldiers inside a siege tower could launch an attack from very close quarters and even climb over the walls to enter an enemy city.

THE TORTOISE FORMATION

Roman army commanders were famous for their brilliant battle tactics, and they used some clever tricks to overcome their enemies. Sometimes, a group of soldiers

Caesar's tortoise attack

What does it tell us?

There are several accounts of the *testudo* (or tortoise formation) being used in battle. The most famous comes in Julius Caesar's description of the Roman invasion of Britain in 55 B.C. Caesar records that his soldiers formed a testudo in order to approach the walls of a British fort. This clever tactic clearly paid off because Caesar states that within a few hours the Roman legions had captured the fort. The picture above shows a reenactment of the famous Roman tortoise formation.

would advance in a formation called a *testudo*—or tortoise. To create this formation, the soldiers locked their shields together to form a solid barrier over their heads and around the front of the group. This "shell" protected them from enemy spears and allowed the soldiers to get very close to the enemy while remaining unharmed.

BUILDING DEFENSES

Once the Roman army had conquered an area, they had to make sure that their lands remained safe from enemy attacks. They built high walls marking the edge of their territory and posted soldiers in forts along the walls to defend the Roman lands. One of the most famous Roman defenses was Hadrian's Wall, which ran across the north of Britain, marking the northernmost edge of the Empire. It was built by the Emperor Hadrian in the second century A.D. in order to keep the warlike northern tribes out of Roman Britain.

Keeping out the enemy: Hadrian's Wall

What does it tell us?

Hadrian's Wall (*shown below*) still runs for 115 miles (185 kilometers) across northern England, south of the present-day border with Scotland. For much of its length, the wall is crowned with a walkway where Roman soldiers would have patrolled night and day. A series of forts, built at intervals along the wall, provided shelter for posted army units. The wall offers dramatic evidence of the difficult task that faced the Romans as they tried to keep their vast Empire safe.

WHAT WAS LIFE LIKE FOR THE ROMANS?

For some fortunate Romans, life was very comfortable. They lived in beautiful town houses or country villas, held lavish banquets, and enjoyed a wide range of leisure activities. Not everyone lived like this, however. Most of the people who lived in the Empire had to work hard to survive.

TOWN LIFE

Roman towns and cities were constructed around grand central squares, which contained impressive public buildings and temples. A network of streets stretched out from these squares. Some streets were wide and flanked by imposing houses that belonged to wealthy citizens. Other streets were much narrower and lined with stores, workshops, and various snack stalls. The poorer people of the town lived above a shop or had rooms in a crowded apartment building.

▲ The ruins of a street in Pompeii, southern Italy, showing the remains of shops and workshops.

The houses of the rich usually had two floors or more. They had painted walls and mosaic floors and were furnished with couches and low tables. Downstairs, the rooms were arranged around a central courtyard and included a dining room, a kitchen, and, sometimes, a bathroom. Family bedrooms were upstairs. Some town houses also had a garden where people could relax and entertain their friends.

Poorer people lived in small, bare rooms with very little furniture. Unlike the rich, they had no running water or toilets, and no places to cook. Roman apartment buildings were not well built, and they often collapsed or caught on fire.

SHOPS AND STALLS

Bakers, butchers, fish dealers, and wine merchants all provided for the citizens' daily needs, and people also visited busy markets, where they could buy milk, cheese, and vegetables brought into town by local farmers. Stalls selling snacks also were very popular because most people in towns did not have a kitchen where they could cook food. Many food staples were imported from conquered lands as the Roman Empire expanded—often competing with local farmers.

A buried town: Pompeii

What does it tell us?

In A.D. 79, the Roman city of Pompeii, in southern Italy, was destroyed by a sudden volcanic eruption. The town was showered by burning ash from Mount Vesuvius, and most of its citizens were killed instantly. Hundreds of years later, archaeologists began to uncover the ruined town and discovered houses, apartments, shops, and workshops— all buried under the ash. They also discovered furniture, tools, jewelry, and toys that had survived almost intact. Today, most of the town has been excavated, and its treasures have been placed in museums. The remains at Pompeii provide a remarkably complete picture of life in a Roman town.

A collection of food containers found in Pompeii. ▶

Buried treasure: glass for the dead

What does it tell us?

Some exquisite glassware has been found in Roman graves. These objects include delicate flasks and bowls made from multicolored glass and inlaid with precious metals. These beautiful objects show how skillful the Roman glassmakers were. They also illustrate some Romans' belief in the afterlife. When they were buried, rich Romans usually were equipped with everything they needed for a comfortable existence beyond the grave.

CRAFT WORKERS

In towns all over the Empire, craft workers labored in workshops to produce a huge variety of goods. Apart from the basic essentials, such as clothes and sandals, pots, pans, and tools, there were also luxury goods. Goldsmiths and silversmiths made elaborate jewelry, glass blowers produced exquisite bowls and goblets, and engravers carved delicate cameo portraits for brooches and rings.

ROMAN BATHS

Very few Roman houses had bathrooms, so people from a variety of social classes in towns paid a daily visit to the public baths. Roman baths, however, were not

▲ The remains of the Roman baths in the city of Bath in southern England, as they look today.

simply a place to have a good wash. Many of them were very grand buildings with their own gardens, shops, and even libraries. People went to the baths to exercise, relax, and meet their friends.

A visit to the baths usually began with vigorous exercise followed by some time in the *calidarium*—a very hot pool. Instead of using soap, the Romans covered their bodies with oil. Then they used a tool, called a *strigil*, to scrape off all the dirt and the oil. Wealthy Romans brought their slaves to the baths so that the slaves could do the scraping for them.

As well as the *calidarium*, there was a steam room and a massage area, where people lay on tables and were massaged with oil. Before they left the baths, bathers gradually cooled down in the *tepidarium*, a lukewarm pool, before taking a refreshing dip in the *frigidarium* —an unheated, open-air pool. After they had finished bathing, people might buy a snack at a food stall, read in the library, or relax in the gardens.

Caracalla's baths

What do they tell us?

Several examples of Roman baths have survived in cities and towns around the Empire. The most impressive baths of all were built in Rome around A.D. 216 by the Emperor Caracalla. This vast leisure complex had room for up to 1,600 people and included art galleries, gymnasiums, gardens, libraries, meeting rooms, and shops. Decorated throughout with statues and mosaics, Caracalla's baths are now in ruins, but tourists may still gain an impression of their massive size.

COUNTRY LIFE

During the time of the Republic, many Roman families owned small farms in the Italian countryside. Families survived by growing grain and olives and keeping a few pigs, sheep, and cattle. By the second century B.C., however, many of these family farms had been abandoned as farmers left the countryside to join the Roman army. The old farming lands were bought by rich landowners, who created huge estates that were farmed by slaves.

By the time of the Empire, almost all farm workers were slaves. They had an exhausting life, planting and harvesting crops with very basic tools, chopping down trees to clear new fields, and looking after animals. Farms provided people in the towns with grain, olive oil, wine, meat, cheese, and wool. Some Roman farms, especially in North Africa, sent their crops overseas to other parts of the Empire, and the owners of these farms often became incredibly rich.

Evidence under foot: floors

What do they tell us?

Although the walls of most Roman villas have disappeared, many floors have survived, buried under layers of earth. When excavated, these floors reveal the layout of a villa's rooms. Many surviving floors are decorated with mosaics, which are often remarkably complete. Roman mosaics often feature geometric patterns; many show legends of the gods or scenes from country life. This floor, with its striking geometric patterns, was discovered in the Roman province of Libya, northern Africa.

▲ One of the most lavish Roman villas was built by the emperor Hadrian at Tivoli, near Rome. It was surrounded by beautiful gardens and two bathhouses that were heated by the hypocaust system.

A VILLA IN THE COUNTRY

For most Roman landowners, their country villas were simply the places to which they escaped when city life became too stressful. Some villas were basic, but others were luxurious, with their own bathhouse and beautiful formal gardens filled with statues and ornamental pools.

Usually, the rooms of a villa were arranged around a central, enclosed garden. The rooms included a dining room, a kitchen, and a study, as well as several bedrooms for family and guests. The back of the villa contained storerooms, estate offices, and living quarters for the farm manager, servants, and slaves. The walls of country villas often were colorfully painted with beautiful frescoes, while their floors were laid with stunning mosaics.

The hypocaust system

What does it tell us?

Underneath the floors of some Roman villas, archaeologists have discovered evidence of an ingenious method of central heating. Known as the hypocaust system, it was powered by a fire in the basement. Hot air from the fire flowed into spaces underneath the floor and inside the villa's walls to heat up the entire house. Roman baths also were heated by the well-designed hypocaust system.

WHAT WERE ROMAN FAMILIES LIKE?

Family life was very important to the Romans. At the head of the family was the father—known as the *paterfamilias*. He led the daily family prayers and made all the big decisions for his family. A typical Roman father, however, also spent a lot of time away from home, leaving his wife to run the household and take care of the children's early education.

During the Roman Republic, most women had large families and stayed at home, teaching their children and spinning and weaving cloth for their families' clothes. By the time of the Empire, though, many wealthy wives

left all the work to their slaves. Instead, they spent most of their time pampering themselves, relaxing, and attending grand dinner parties.

ROMAN CHILDREN

Most children living in the Empire were brought up to be loyal Roman citizens. Boys from wealthy families were trained as soldiers or to work in government; girls were prepared to be good wives. The children of traders and craft workers

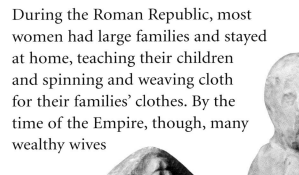

Having fun: Roman toys

What do they tell us?

Archaeologists have discovered several Roman toys, including a simple doll, some glass and pottery marbles, and some toy animals. There also is evidence that Roman children played on seesaws and swings, practiced fighting with wooden swords, and even had miniature chariots that were pulled by goats or geese. The toy horse shown here could have been pushed or pulled along.

learned the family trade by copying their parents. Children from poor families started work as soon as they could, but richer parents sent their children to school.

LIFE AS A SLAVE

Many Roman families had slaves to do the hard work in their homes. Household slaves did the shopping, cooking, and cleaning. They also served at meals and helped their mistress with her hair, clothes, and makeup. Other slaves worked in shops and businesses or on farms.

Slaves usually were bought from dealers or were born into a slave family. They had no legal rights and belonged entirely to their master or mistress. In many Roman homes, however, slaves were treated kindly, despite their lack of freedom. Educated slaves worked, in some instances, as private tutors, doctors, or librarians, and some were employed as government officials.

Life was not so pleasant for other slaves. Many were forced to do hard and dangerous work in mines or on building sites. Others were trained as gladiators and had to fight to the death in the arena for public entertainment.

A slave serving ▶ at a banquet, shown in a Roman mosaic.

WHAT DID THE ROMANS WEAR?

Most Roman clothes were very simple. They usually were made from wool, which was spun and woven by hand at home or in a workshop. Sometimes, the Romans wore clothes made from Egyptian linen, and some very rich people had garments made from Indian cotton or Chinese silk. Both men and women wore many rings and fastened their clothes with brooches. Wealthy women also adorned themselves with gold and silver bracelets, jeweled necklaces, and earrings.

MEN'S CLOTHES

The basic garment for men was a simple belted tunic that was made from two rectangles of wool stitched together. Under this tunic, a man wore a loincloth made from a strip of wool or linen. Men also wore simple cloaks that could be wrapped around them or fastened at the neck with a brooch.

For special occasions, men and boys wore a toga over a tunic. A toga was a very long strip of woolen cloth that wrapped around the body and draped over one shoulder. Togas were usually plain white, but, until they were sixteen, boys from wealthy families wore a white toga with a narrow purple border. Senators wore togas with a broad, purple border.

Unisex jewelry: Roman rings

What do they tell us?

Many Roman rings have survived—especially in graves. These rings were worn by men as well as women. Wealthy Romans wore rings made from gold and silver set with precious stones, while rings made from bronze have been discovered in the graves of poorer people. Some Roman rings were carved from semiprecious stones, such as the amber ring shown here.

WOMEN'S CLOTHES

Roman women wore a long, belted, sleeveless dress called a *stola*. Over this was a large rectangular shawl, known as a *palla*, which could be worn draped around the shoulders or looped over the head, like a hood. Under the stola, women wore a loincloth and sometimes a simple leather bra. Girls wore white until they were married, but after marriage they often wore brightly colored stolas.

Early portraits: coffins from Egypt

What do they tell us?

In the Roman province of Egypt, people were buried in wooden coffins with their portraits painted on the lid, like the one shown here. Several of these coffins have been discovered in the dry sands of Egypt. The coffin portraits are very lifelike and detailed. They provide valuable evidence of what Roman jewelry, hairstyles, clothing, and even makeup were like.

BEAUTY CARE

Looking good was very important to the Romans, and both men and women liked to take good care of themselves. By the time of the Empire, many wealthy Roman women were spending hours every morning being made up by their slaves, and most men started the day by visiting the barber's shop for a shave.

ROMAN MAKEUP

It was very fashionable in Roman times for women to look pale, so they whitened their faces and arms with powdered chalk or a mixture made from lead that turned out to be poisonous. They darkened their eyebrows and eyelashes with soot, and painted their lips red, using plant dye or the sediment of red wine. As well as applying makeup, Roman women liked to treat their skin with a variety of preparations. They applied face masks of bread soaked in milk and even used a cream made from crushed snails.

HAIR CARE

During the time of the Republic, most women wore their hair tied in a simple bun at the back of their head, but by the time of the Empire some very elaborate styles had developed. Wealthy women's hair was curled, braided and held in place with dozens of pins. Some women even cut off their slaves' hair and had it made into wigs or hairpieces for themselves.

Ancient makeup: Roman cosmetic equipment

What does it tell us?

A range of cosmetics has survived from the time of the Roman Empire, showing the care that some Roman women lavished on their appearance. Archaeologists have found delicate glass pots and jars for holding oils, creams, and perfumes. They have also discovered some slender silver spatulas, which were used for mixing and applying cosmetics.

◀ Long-handled spoons like this were used by Roman slaves to prepare cosmetics for their mistresses.

Most Roman men kept their hair short, either combed forward or curled. They usually were clean shaven, although in the later Empire, the Emperor Hadrian started a fashion for beards. Some men and women tried to prevent their hair from going gray by applying a paste made of earthworms and herbs, while others used a brown hair dye made from walnut shells and wild onions.

Changing styles: Roman statues

What do they tell us?

Statues of men and women from throughout the Roman period give a very clear idea of changing hairstyles. Some of the statues of women, dating from the second century A.D., show some very extreme styles, with hair piled up at the front in a mountain of curls.

WHAT DID THE ROMANS EAT?

Many of the foods we eat today were unheard of in Roman times. The Romans had no potatoes or tomatoes, and their basic foods probably were bread and beans. Rich people had a varied diet, and cooks served up amazing dishes at banquets, but poor people's food was very plain and simple.

Poor people and slaves survived on porridge, bread, and soup, but richer Romans had more interesting meals. For breakfast, they would often eat a snack of bread with honey, and lunch was usually a simple meal of eggs, cheese, cold meat, and fruit. Most wealthier Romans ate little during the day, waiting instead to eat their main meal. This supper usually consisted of roasted poultry or fish, accompanied by lentils or other beans. The Romans drank a lot of wine, which

Roman tableware

What does it tell us?

A wide variety of pots and dishes have survived from Roman times, showing how Romans of all classes served and ate their food. Dishes range from basic polished red pots, known as Samian ware, to elaborate bowls and goblets made from silver and glass. The cup shown above is decorated with a scene from a banquet.

they usually flavored with spices or sweetened with honey, and diluted with water. Poorer Romans drank water from the public fountains or from streams.

Buried kitchen: evidence from Pompeii

What does it tell us?

When archaeologists uncovered the ruins of a large house in the buried city of Pompeii, they found the remains of a complete kitchen (*shown below*). This provided fascinating evidence of the way the Romans prepared and cooked their meals. The kitchen had a stone cooking stove with a set of cooking pots still standing on it. The bronze pots were heated by burning charcoal chips in a shallow tray beneath them.

LAVISH BANQUETS

Wealthy Romans had trained cooks who produced lavish banquets with many courses. Cooks competed with each other to produce exotic dishes, serving up food such as larks' tongues, mice cooked in honey, and even elephants' trunks. Rich sauces were especially popular—probably because they helped to disguise the taste of food that wasn't very fresh.

Banquets lasted for hours and included many courses, which were presented in spectacular ways. Sometimes, guests ate so much that they had to visit a small side room, called a *vomitarium*, to vomit up some of their food!

The Colosseum

What does it tell us?

The remains of several Roman amphitheaters have been discovered in Europe and Asia, but the biggest one of all is the Colosseum in Rome, which could hold 50,000 people. It is still possible to see its tiered seats and the small cells under the arena where prisoners and wild animals were kept.

HAVING FUN

By the time of the Empire, many people had a great deal of free time because their slaves did most of the work. For entertainment, people flocked to watch bloody shows, known as "the games," and also enjoyed chariot races and theater performances.

The Roman emperors paid for spectacular public shows, which were held in vast public amphitheaters such as the Colosseum in Rome. The games featured musicians, dancers, jugglers, and performing animals. Sometimes, wild beasts were released into the arena and hunted down with spears, daggers, and bows and arrows; sometimes the arena was flooded with water for mock sea battles.

Perhaps the greatest attractions of the games were the gladiator fights. Most gladiators were slaves, criminals, or prisoners of war. Some female slaves also were forced to fight. The gladiators dressed in skimpy armor and fought each other in savage battles that often ended in death.

RACES AND PLAYS

Chariot races were another major attraction. In a chariot race, teams of horses each pulled a chariot around a race track while the crowd cheered wildly for their favorite team. The races were incredibly wild and dangerous, and drivers and their horses often were killed.

As well as attending the games and the races, the Romans also loved to go to the theater. Plays usually were shown in outdoor stone theaters with rows of tiered seats. At first, the Romans mainly performed Latin versions of ancient Greek comedies and tragedies, but later they invented pantomime—a more popular form of theater. In these simple productions, a chorus sang a series of songs while the actors mimed the action.

Funny faces: actors' masks

What do they tell us?

Roman plays were acted by an all-male cast, and the actors wore masks to indicate the type of character they were playing. Some mosaics and carvings of actors' masks have survived, providing a good idea of what a Roman audience would have seen. The masks are simple and dramatic so that they can be seen from anywhere in the theater. They show typical characters that an actor might play, ranging from "the virtuous maiden," "the wise old man," or "the smiling fool" to gods and heroes. The mask (*above*) comes from a mosaic decoration for a Roman theater.

HOW DID THE ROMANS COMMUNICATE?

By the fifth century B.C., some leading members of the Latin people knew how to read and write. The Latins learned their reading and writing skills from their northern neighbors, the Etruscans. The Latins also were strongly influenced by the Greeks and included many Greek words in their language.

By the time the Latins founded Rome, around 750 B.C., they had developed a language of their own, called Latin. Gradually, Latin spread throughout Italy. It also spread throughout the Roman Empire, where it became the official language of government.

READING AND WRITING

Although the vast majority of people in the Roman Empire could not read or write, wealthy families all over the Empire made sure their children had a good education. This meant learning to read and write Latin. People took pride in their ability to read, and the works of authors who wrote in Latin were widely enjoyed.

School began when a child was seven years old. Girls and boys were taught together in a primary school called a *ludus*, where they learned reading, writing, and arithmetic. Pupils learned to write on reusable wax tablets, using a pointed metal pen called a stylus. At the age of eleven, girls left school, but most boys moved on to a secondary

Pride in writing

What does it tell us?

This portrait found in the city of Pompeii illustrates how important writing was to the Romans. It shows a young couple who clearly wish to show the world that they are both educated. The man holds a rolled-up papyrus scroll, and may be a lawyer. The woman holds up her stylus and wax tablet, showing that she too enjoys writing.

school, known as a *grammaticus*. Here, pupils studied Greek and Roman literature, mathematics, history, geography, and music. Making speeches was very important in Roman public life, so boys also studied the art of public speaking, which was known as rhetoric.

▲ Children throughout the Roman Empire were taught to read and write Latin. A variation of the Latin alphabet, roman, is the form we now use in Western writing.

Different texts: Roman writing materials

What do they tell us?

Archaeologists have found a range of writing materials, showing that the Romans used different methods for different types of writing. For unimportant texts, people either used a stylus to write on wax tablets or wrote with a pen and ink on cheap, thin slices of wood. Legal contracts were written on Egyptian papyrus (a type of paper made from reeds). The most important texts—such as works of literature—were written on vellum. Vellum was made from a thin layer of calf's skin and had a very smooth surface. By the end of the Roman period, vellum pages were sewn together to make books that were protected by leather covers.

RUNNING THE EMPIRE

Within the vast Roman Empire, people spoke many different languages, but everyone was united by the common language of Latin. All over the Empire, Latin was the language used by lawyers, government officials, and tax collectors. This official language of government made the task of running the Roman Empire much easier.

SENDING MESSAGES

The smooth running of the Roman Empire also depended on a very efficient transportation system. Roman ships made regular journeys from Italy across the Mediterranean Sea, reaching Constantinople, Northern Africa, and Spain, and a vast network of roads covered the Empire.

Built to last: Roman roads

What do they tell us?

Roman roads were so well built that many of them were in daily use until the eighteenth century. Even today, some stretches survive, showing how the Romans built their roads. First, a wide trench was dug and filled with sand. A layer of gravel and stones was packed down firmly over the sand. Finally, large, flat paving stones were laid over the surface of the road, and its edges were marked out with rectangular stone blocks. The road shown above is the Appian Way, which ran south through Italy from Rome.

Roman engineers designed their roads to be as direct as possible. Sometimes, when a road reached a wide, deep valley, the Romans constructed a raised road, called a viaduct, which ran right over the valley. They also built massive, arched bridges to span wide rivers.

Roman roads were even and well-paved, and the Romans made sure they were kept in good repair. Good roads meant that messengers from all parts of the Empire could quickly carry news of any trouble to Rome. In response, a unit of soldiers could be sent to march straight to the trouble spot. Milestones were placed at regular intervals along the roads so that travelers could see how far they had to go to reach their destination.

This Roman milestone still stands ▶ in Capernaum, Israel, with part of its original inscription still intact.

Pliny's letters

What do they tell us?

The Romans were great letter writers, and many letters survive from Roman times. The most famous Roman letter writer was Pliny the Younger, who lived from about A.D. 61 to 113. Pliny's letters include his correspondence with the Emperor Trajan and also many personal messages to his wife and friends. His best known letter describes the volcanic eruption of Mount Vesuvius, which destroyed the city of Pompeii and killed his uncle, Pliny the Elder.

WHO DID THE ROMANS WORSHIP?

U p until the time of the late Empire, most Romans worshipped a range of different gods. Some were grand figures, such as Apollo, the god of the Sun. Others were friendly household spirits who, the Romans believed, kept watch over their homes. In the Roman provinces of the Middle East, many people followed the Jewish religion. Other people worshipped gods from Persia or Egypt, such as Mithras or Isis. By the fourth century A.D., however, the most popular religion in the Roman Empire was the relatively new faith of Christianity.

MIGHTY GODS

Before the coming of Christianity, most Romans prayed to a group of powerful gods and goddesses who had first been worshipped by the Greeks. Chief among these gods were Jupiter, the god of the sky, and his wife Juno, the goddess of women. Each god or goddess was responsible for a different area of life.

Places of worship: Roman temples

What do they tell us?

Several Roman temples have survived in the city of Rome and the Roman provinces. These impressive buildings show how a public temple was laid out. At the front of the temple, wide steps lead to a covered area where priests offered sacrifices to the god to whom the temple was dedicated. At the back was a private room, which was the sacred part of the temple. The statue of the god was kept here. Only priests were allowed in this area. The temple shown here was dedicated to Portumnus, the god of harbors and ports. It was built on the banks of the Tiber River, in Rome, around the year 100 B.C.

Legends of the gods: Ovid's poems

What do they tell us?

During the first century A.D., the Roman poet Ovid wrote a series of poems based on the legends of the gods. One of the most famous of these poems tells how the goddess Juno turned Ariadne, the weaver, into a spider as a punishment for daring to love the great god Jupiter. Ovid's poems were widely read in Roman times, and they reveal the richness of the Roman legends.

The Romans prayed to Mars (the god of war) for victory in battle and asked Venus to grant them success in love. As well as saying prayers, the Romans sacrificed animals to the gods.

Priests slaughtered oxen, sheep, pigs, and doves on open-air altars in front of temples. After a creature was killed, its internal organs were taken out and examined. The Romans believed that the pattern made by the organs helped them discover the will of the gods.

The chief Roman god ▶ was Jupiter, who was also the god of thunder and lightning. Romans believed that when he was angry, he hurled thunderbolts from the sky.

ROMAN PRIESTS

Many Roman priests had other jobs as well, and the chief priest was the emperor himself. In contrast, one group of priestesses, known as the vestal virgins, devoted most of their lives to serving their goddess. Vestal virgins were chosen at the age of seven and spent the next thirty years living in the temple of Vesta in Rome. Vesta was the goddess of Earth, and it was the vestal virgins' sacred duty to keep a fire constantly burning in her temple. The Romans believed that disaster would strike the state if this fire were ever allowed to go out.

GOD OF HEALING

One of the Romans' favorite gods was Aesculapias, the god of healing. Medicine was not very advanced in Roman times, so people often asked the gods to cure them of their diseases. Some people were so desperate for cures that they spent all night in the temple of Aesculapias in Rome.

Asking for help: votive offerings

What do they tell us?

Many small gifts, known as votive offerings, have been discovered in Roman temples dedicated to the god of healing. Offerings take the form of metal plaques or stone carvings of parts that needed a cure: ears, legs, or eyes, as shown here. Experts believe these gifts were either to thank for a cure, or to remind the god of the request for healing.

Worship at home: a household shrine

What does it tell us?

Archaeologists have discovered several household shrines inside Roman homes. One of these shrines was found in a house at Pompeii. It consists of a simple niche in the wall with a small, stone altar. On the altar stood a group of statuettes, representing the household gods, while a pot found in front of the altar originally may have contained an offering to these gods.

HOUSEHOLD GODS

Not all worship in Roman times was carried out by priests in temples. In their own homes, the Romans worshipped two kinds of gods whom they believed looked after their households. The *lares* were spirits who protected the home, while the *penates* looked after the larder and the food stores.

Each Roman house had its own shrine where the family held daily prayers. It was called the *lararium*, and it contained small statues of the lares and penates. Here, Roman families offered food, wine, and flowers to their household gods. On special occasions, such as birthdays and weddings, the lares and penates were given extra gifts.

GODS FROM FOREIGN LANDS

By the first century A.D., many Romans were losing respect for the old gods and goddesses, most of whom they had taken from the Greeks. As their conquests brought Romans into contact with religions of other cultures, many took up foreign faiths. These faiths had strict rules on how people should live and also offered their followers the promise of salvation and life in heaven after death.

ISIS AND MITHRAS

Two of the most popular gods from foreign countries were Isis, from Egypt, and Mithras, from Persia. Thousands of Roman women became passionate followers of Isis after the Egyptian Queen Cleopatra spent a year in Rome in 45 B.C. The Persian god Mithras was especially popular with Roman soldiers. Followers of Mithras gathered in underground temples where they suffered terrifying tests, such as being locked in a coffin for hours.

Religious rattle: a priest's sistrum

What does it tell us?

Several metal rattles have been found in ruined Roman temples devoted to the Egyptian goddess Isis. Carvings (*such as the one shown here*) of ceremonies indicate that priests shook a rattle, known as a sistrum, during their services. The rattles produced a delicate, clinking sound.

JEWS AND CHRISTIANS

In the area of the Roman Empire that is now the Middle East, many people followed the ancient religion of Judaism. Then, around A.D. 30, the new religion of Christianity began to spread from Jerusalem. Both Jews and Christians believed that there is only one God, which meant they could not worship Roman gods as well. This led the Roman emperors to conduct fierce campaigns against the Jews and Christians. Emperor Hadrian tried to stamp out Judaism completely. Nero sent hundreds of Christians to the arena to be torn apart by wild beasts, and Emperor Diocletian had thousands of people executed for refusing to give up their Christian faith.

THE RISE OF CHRISTIANITY

In A.D. 312, Emperor Constantine converted to Christianity and allowed Christians to worship freely. In A.D. 391,

Christianity was declared the official religion of the Roman Empire. By the end of the fourth century, Christian monasteries and churches were being built throughout the Empire.

Christian catacombs

What do they tell us?

Archaeologists working in the city of Rome have discovered a series of underground chapels, in which early Christians met to worship in secret. Known as the catacombs, they originally were used as burial chambers. Some of the catacombs still have stone altars and the remains of Bible scenes painted on their walls. They provide a vivid impression of the way the early Christians worshipped.

WHAT DID THE ROMANS CONTRIBUTE TO THE WORLD?

▲ This nineteenth-century illustration shows flowers with their Latin names beside them.

The Romans had an enormous impact on the world. Even though the Roman Empire came to an end over 1,500 years ago, people still use Latin words every day. Architects design buildings in the Roman style, and modern city life owes a great deal to the Romans. Lawyers and politicians today still follow some ancient Roman practices, and some Christmas traditions and modern wedding celebrations (*see page 45*) are based on Roman festivals.

USING LATIN

After the Roman Empire collapsed in A.D. 476, the Roman Catholic Church kept the Latin language alive. Church services were held in Latin, and monks hand-copied a range of Roman texts. For hundreds of years, people have studied authors who wrote in Latin, and some children today still learn Latin in school. Scientists give Latin names to animals and plants. The use of this common scientific language means that the same names can be used all over the world.

LATIN ROOTS

By the time the Roman Empire came to an end, Latin was the official language of the Empire. All the languages spoken in the Roman Empire were influenced by Latin. Italian, French, and Spanish all come directly from Latin. They are called Romance languages, referring to Rome. Even the English language, which is not closely related to Latin, includes many words with Latin roots. For example, the English word *school* comes from the Latin word *schola*. English also uses Latin phrases in daily speech—such as *et cetera*, which means "and the rest." Romans spread their language and writing system as they conquered neighboring lands, especially Spain and France, while Latin gradually changed into Italian in Italy.

ROMAN LETTERS AND MONTHS CONTINUE

Of the twenty-six letters in the Western alphabet, twenty-two come from the Roman alphabet. The Romans had no *W* or *Y*. They used the letter *V* for *U* and *V*, and *I* and *J* were both written as *I*.

Most of our months have Roman names. March is named after Mars, the god of war, and June gets its name from the goddess Juno. In the Roman calendar, September, October, November, and December were originally the seventh, eighth, ninth, and tenth months of the year. The months of July and August were named after Julius Caesar and the Emperor Augustus. All these names suggest that our calendar is based on a Roman system.

Roman numerals survive: dates and hours

What do they tell us?

The numbers we use today are based on Arabic numerals, which are much easier to use than Roman numerals. The practice of using Roman numerals has not died out completely, though. Dates are still sometimes shown in Roman numerals, and some clock faces also have numerals in the Roman style, as shown on the pocket watch below.

LAWYERS AND SENATORS

In most Roman courts, cases were tried by a judge and a jury, and this type of trial has been copied all over the world. Roman lawyers also wrote down a vast set of laws, and these have provided the models for many modern laws.

As well as copying Roman laws, people have been influenced by the Roman method of government—especially that of the Roman Republic. After the American Revolution, many Americans saw the Roman Republic as a shining example of a state without a king. They set up a republic with a senate and senators and based their senate on the Roman senate at the time of the Roman Republic.

BUILDING LIKE THE ROMANS

After the Roman Empire collapsed, many cities fell into ruin, and the secrets of the Roman builders were almost forgotten. By the fifteenth century, however, many architects in Italy became very interested in Roman architecture. They copied the Romans and constructed grand public buildings with massive columns and rounded arches. This impressive style

The Pont du Gard aqueduct

What does it tell us?

The Pont du Gard in southern France is part of an elaborate Roman water system (or aqueduct) that carried water from the mountains to the city of Nimes. It consists of three layers of arches, built one above the other, with a channel for water running along the top. The Pont du Gard has survived for over two thousand years; it provides a stunning example of the skill of Roman engineers. Centuries later, modern city planners still copy the methods used by the Roman aqueduct builders.

▲ Ever since the fifteenth century, people have built grand structures in the Roman style. The Arc de Triomphe in Paris is modeled after a Roman victory arch.

was very popular, and it soon spread throughout Europe.

ANCIENT CELEBRATIONS

Many of our present-day celebrations have their origins in ancient Rome. For example, the way we celebrate Christmas today is partly based on the Roman feast of Saturnalia. At this midwinter feast, people cooked huge meals, played games, and exchanged gifts. Today's wedding customs are strongly influenced by the Romans: When a Roman couple became engaged, the girl was given a ring to wear on the third finger of her left hand. On her wedding day, the bride wore a white dress and a garland of flowers in her hair.

LIVING LIKE THE ROMANS

Many of our towns and cities follow the Roman pattern, with grand public buildings in the center and streets laid out in a regular grid. Our roads and sewage and water systems are similar to those built by the Romans. People live in houses with central heating, eat food in snack shops, and visit public swimming pools and vast sports arenas—just as the Romans did two thousand years ago. The Roman Empire still influences us today.

TIME LINE

FIND OUT MORE

BOOKS

Chandler, Fiona, and Sam Taplin, Jane Bingham.
The Usborne Encyclopedia of the Roman World.
Usborne, 2001.

Deary, Terry. *Rotten Romans.* Horrible Histories
(series). Scholastic, 1997.

James, Simon. *Ancient Rome.* Eyewitness Books
(series). Dorling Kindersley, 1990.

Solway, Andrew and Stephen Biesty. *Rome.*
Oxford University Press, 2003.

Watkins, Richard. *Gladiator.* Houghton Mifflin,
2000.

WEB SITES

www.bbc.co.uk/schools/romans/
Designed especially for schools, this BBC site
includes activities and suggestions for "More
to explore."

www.crystalinks.com/romearchitecture.html
Enjoy stunning photographs and interesting
facts about ancient Roman sites.

www.pbs.org/empires/romans/
This American Public Broadcasting Service site
provides an in-depth look at the Roman world,
life in Roman times, and a detailed time line.

www.roman-empire.net/
Explore the Roman Empire in sections on
Roman place names, maps, pictures from Rome,
and photographs of battle reenactments.

www.romans-in-britain.org.uk/
Learn more with this overview of Roman sites in
Britain and biographies of key figures.

GLOSSARY

amphitheater—a large, stone, circular building with many seats, where people went to watch gladiator fights

arena—the central area or stage of an amphitheater

breastplate—a layer of armor made from metal or leather that was strapped onto a soldier's chest for protection

cavalry—soldiers who ride horses

centurion—an officer in the Roman army who led a group of soldiers called a *century*

chariot—a horse-drawn vehicle with two or four wheels, used for races, battles, and parades

colony—land that is controlled by rulers from a foreign country; the Romans had many colonies, which were all ruled from Rome

conquer—to overcome an enemy and win land

consul—during the Roman Republic, consuls were the leaders of the government (senate)

council—a group of important people, elected or appointed, who meet together to make plans about how to run their country

empire—all the lands that were controlled by the Romans. The term *Roman Empire* also refers to the period from 27 B.C. to A.D. 476, when Rome was ruled by emperors

fresco—a picture painted on a wall while the plaster is still damp

gladiator—someone who was trained to fight in an arena to entertain the Roman people; gladiators often were slaves

governor—someone who ran a province (or region) in the Roman Empire

legion—a large unit of soldiers; legionnaires usually were foot soldiers

loincloth—a piece of cloth used to cover the waist and hips

mosaic—a picture made up of hundreds of small pieces of stone, marble, or glass

philosopher—someone who thinks very carefully about human life and how it should be lived

province—a region of the Roman Empire outside Italy that was ruled by a governor

republic—a country without a king or a queen, whose rulers are elected by the people. The Roman Republic lasted from 510 B.C. to 27 B.C.

senate—the group of men who governed Rome during the Roman Republic

senator—a member of the senate

stylus—a thin metal rod, used like a pen to write on a wax tablet

toga—a long piece of cloth, worn by Roman men, that was draped around the body

tribe—a group of people who share the same descendants, laws, and customs

villa—a large, comfortable Roman house in the country

votive offering—a gift offered to a god, in hope that a special request or prayer will be granted or answered

INDEX

OLD BETHEL WEEKDAY

OLD BETHEL WEEKDAY SCHOOL
7995 EAST 21ST STREET
INDIANAPOLIS IN 46219

THE ADOPTED ONE

Library of Congress Cataloging in Publication Data

Stein, Sara Bonnett.
    The adopted one.

    SUMMARY: Includes dual text, one for the adult reader,
one for the child, explaining some of the conflicting
feelings of an adopted child.
    1. Adoption. [1. Adoption] I. Title.
HV875.S695 1979   362.7'34   78-19688
ISBN 0-8027-6346-4

First published in the United States of America in
1979 by the Walker Publishing Company, Inc.

Published simultaneously in Canada by Beaver-
books, Limited, Pickering, Ontario

ISBN 0-8027-6346-4

Library of Congress Catalog Card Number
78-19688

Printed in the United States of America

THE ADOPTED ONE

An Open Family Book For Parents And Children Together

by Sara Bonnett Stein

Thomas R. Holman,
Ph.D., Consultant
Psychologist, Postgraduate Center
for Mental Health, New York, New York

Photographs by Erika Stone

Walker and Company
New York, New York
Created by Media Projects Incorporated

A Note About This Book

When your child was a baby, you took him to the doctor to have him immunized for childhood illnesses. The injections hurt a little, but you knew they would prepare his body to cope with far more serious threats in the future. Yet there are other threats as painful and destructive to a child's growth as physical illness: separation from his parents, a death in the family, a new baby, fears and fantasies of his own imagining that hurt as much as pain itself. These Open Family Books are to help adults prepare children for common hurts of childhood.

Caring adults try to protect their child from difficult events. But still that child has ears that overhear, eyes that read the faces of adults around him. If people are sad, he knows it. If people are worried, he knows it. If people are angry, he knows that too.

What he doesn't know—if no one tells him—is the whole story. In his attempts to make sense of what is going on around him, he fills in the fragments he has noticed with fantasied explanations of his own which, because he is a child, are often more frightening than the truth.

We protect children because we know them to be different, more easily damaged than ourselves. But the difference we sense is not widely understood. Children are more easily damaged because they cannot make distinctions yet between what is real and what is unreal, what is magic and what is logic. The tiger under a child's bed at night is as real to him as the tiger in the zoo. When he wishes a bad thing, he believes his wish can make the bad thing happen. His fearful imagining about what is going on grips him because he has no way to test the truth of it.

It is the job of parents to support and explain reality, to guide a child toward the truth even if it is painful. The dose may be small, just as a dose of vaccine is adjusted to the smallness of a baby; but even if it is a little at a time, it is only straightforwardness that gives children the internal strength to deal with things not as they imagine them to be, but as they are.

To do that, parents need to understand what sorts of fears, fantasies, misunderstandings are common to early childhood—what they might expect at three years old, or at five, or seven. They need simpler ways to explain the way complicated things are. The adult text of each of these books, in the left-hand column, explains extraordinary ways that ordinary children between three and eight years old attempt to make sense of difficult events in their lives. It puts into words uncomplicated ways to say things. It is probably best to read the adult text several times before you read the book to your child, so you will get a comfortable feel for the ideas and so you won't be distracted as you talk together. If your child can read, he may one day be curious to read the adult text. That's all right. What's written there is the same as what you are talking about together. The pictures and the words in large print are to start the talking between you and your child. The stories are intense enough to arouse curiosity and feeling. But they are reasonable, forthright and gentle, so a child can deal with the material at whatever level he is ready for.

The themes in these Open Family Books are common to children's play. That is no accident. Play, joyous but also serious, is the way a child enacts himself a little bit at a time, to get used to events, thoughts and feelings he is confused about. Helping a child keep clear on the difference between what is real and what is fantasy will not restrict a child's creativity in play. It will let him use fantasy more freely because it is less frightening.

In some ways, these books won't work. No matter how a parent explains things, a child will misunderstand some part of the explanation, sometimes right away, sometimes in retrospect, weeks or even months later. Parents really can't help this fact of psychological life. Nothing in human growing works all at once, completely or forever. But parents can keep the channels of communication open so that gradually their growing child can bring his version of the way things are closer to the reality. Each time you read an Open Family Book and talk about it together, your child will take in what at that moment is most useful to him. Another day, another month, years later, other aspects of the book will be useful to him in quite different ways. The book will not have changed; what he needs, what he notices, how he uses it will change.

But that is what these books are for: to open between adult and child the potential for growth that exists in human beings of all ages.

We do not accurately know how many children are adopted into or raised by families that are not related by birth. We probably all know of at least one, more likely several adopted or foster children in our own families or neighborhood. Being raised in a family not tied by birth is common. Fictional accounts of adoption are common too. The humble peasant foster family and the wicked stepparent throng the pages of myth and fairy tale. *The Little Princess, Oliver Twist, The Prince and the Pauper* are only a few of the tales of orphans and of parent exchange that stamp the theme into our culture. Moreover, extraordinary as it seems, a startling number of natural children either wish or fear that they are adopted although they are repeatedly assured that is not the case.

Clearly adoption is more than a pragmatic solution to a social problem. To understand the fantasies and feelings of the adopted child is to understand powerful notions that grow from the common predicament of childhood itself.

All of Joshua's family come together for Thanksgiving.
Here comes Aunt Jane and Uncle Henry with Liz and Cathy.

Here comes Aunt Sally and Uncle Sam with Mark and Eric, John and David.

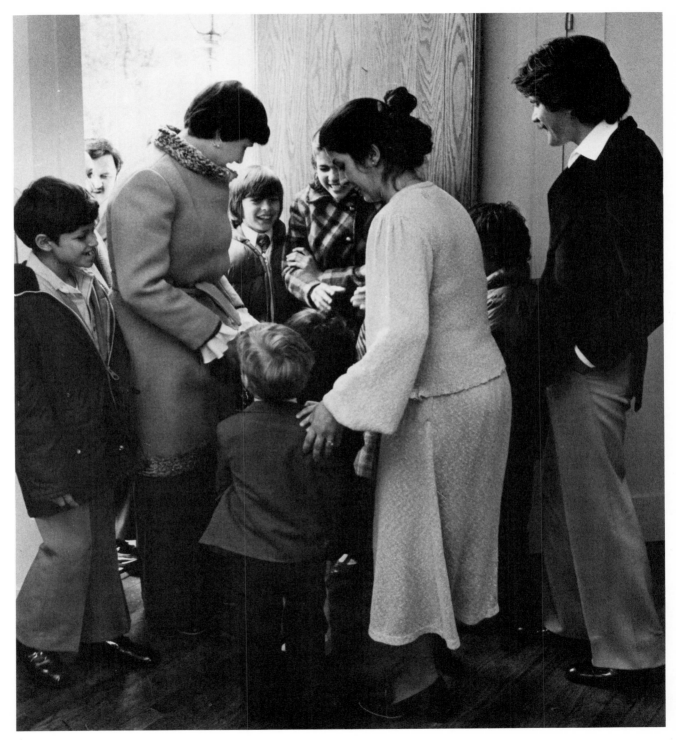

When a baby is born into a family, he is welcomed by a comical little game: He looks just like his daddy; no, his chin is surely Mama's; but those eyebrows are certainly from Grandpa's side of the family.

From the very beginning an adoptive family is made aware of the child's unrelatedness. The child may not look like them. Adults can deal with this. The family's delight—and their understanding that the bond between parent and child is built on love, trust and obligation rather than on blood—rises above small details like matching eyebrows.

As an adopted child becomes aware of his physical differences, however, it is another story. Though eventually he will create his own resemblance by mimicking his parents' facial expressions and postures, it takes time. Right now, here is this whole dark-haired family. Here is Joshua—blond. A child who has his daddy's curly hair and his mommy's hazel eyes is already partly Daddy and partly Mommy. He can look at them and know something of who he is. Joshua has no such mirror. His identification with his parents and relatives will have to be built from less simple, less literal sources.

They all look like one another.
They have black hair.
Joshua doesn't look like them. His hair is blond.
Joshua is adopted.

Another resource that Joshua lacks is the story of his birth. Children love to hear, and to hear again and again, how they kicked and hiccupped, how the cat, accustomed to sleeping on Mommy's belly, objected to such commotion. They giggle to know they made peepee right on the doctor as they were born, or obstinately preferred to suck their tongue instead of the nipple that first day. These stories prove an original organic bond—as children see it, an inside-the-tummy, belly-button-to-belly-button tie of the flesh.

There's even more importance to the story than this. Often, the tale implies a mythic sort of specialness, a portent of later personality. You can probably remember attaching some special meaning to a remark the doctor made, or the timing of a birth, or the singular behavior of a newborn babe.

Adoptive parents may have no information to supply about the period before birth or from a few days to months afterwards. Still, there are ways they can work with what they have.

They talk about being born. "I was in my mommy's belly," Cathy giggles. "I kicked and kicked, and out I came." "I was born backwards," says Liz. "The first thing Daddy saw was my behind."

Parents can, for instance, assure their adopted child that he did not come out of the blue. Like every child, Joshua grew inside the warm comfort of a woman's belly. Surely he, like other babies, cried and cried to leave so comforting a place. Surely the doctor held him upside down, patted his bottom, wiped him dry and wrapped him warmly. His birth certificate tells exactly the day and hour of his birth, and you can re-member as exactly what you were doing that day, what a thunder-storm there was, and how, by strange coincidence, you had just then thought or said . . . it doesn't matter what; any detail can make a myth.

So slight elaboration bears special messages to an adopted child. First, it acknowledges an original hurt, which, though shared by all babies, is particularly poignant to an adopted one: he has had to bear that wrenching separation of mother from baby at birth. And second, it reassures him that, permanent as that separation from his biological mother was in his case, care was taken right away to give him other warmth, other comforts, and another mother.

Joshua has nothing to say. He doesn't know how he was born. He doesn't know the mother who gave birth to him.

"Real" is a deceptive word. We know what Joshua means, but as adults we must clearly recognize that parenting is an active, ongoing behavior. Psychologically, Joshua's adoptive parents are much more real than his biological ones.

Firmly grasping the fact of our realness—and trusting our child will come to see it too—we can go on to help him deal with the question in his own, simpler terms. To tell the truth is the only way we know. To enable parents to tell what they know without compromising the biological mother, the only information usually made available is social status, ethnic and medical background. If more information is made available, it may place adoptive parents in a difficult predicament. On the one hand, they are tugged by their child's thirst to know who his biological parents were. And on the other hand, they fear an eventual search—with its nearly inevitable disappointments—and know their obligation to protect the biological parents.

What follows here is one mother's way of offering her child an acceptable but untraceable image of his natural parents. The photographs are blurred, the faces not visible. You can explain why to your child: It is because no matter how hard an adopted child tries to imagine his parents of birth, he will never be able to see them clearly. He can think about them, but he cannot know them.

"Who is my real mother?" he asks Mommy.

"I'll tell you what I know," his mommy answers.

15

The images here are based on probability. Most babies given in adoption are born to very young women, often teen-agers. The relationship that resulted in pregnancy is frequently sincere and needful, arising in loneliness and confusion. For instance, many teen-age couples report that the reason they did not protect themselves from pregnancy was that contraception interfered with their sense of closeness to one another. Further, they do not give up their babies for adoption without grave conflict and pain. The same loneliness that started a baby also overwhelms the mother with a wish to keep it. The young father, too, only recently the subject of counseling, suffers longing and guilt. Only steady support and insistent pragmatism help these children to give up their babies. Even with help, only one in ten are able to do so. As far as is known, the pain and conflict are never completely resolved.

"I don't know her name. But maybe she was very young. Maybe she still went to school. Maybe she loved a boy. And together they started a baby growing in her belly.

"But they must have been worried and scared. They would have no one to care for the baby when they were in school. They would have no money to buy the baby food and clothes and presents. They must have cried.

Joshua's adoptive mother has suffered too. It is important that Joshua know it. Here were two women grieving, one because she couldn't take care of the baby she gave birth to, the other because she couldn't give birth to the baby she could care for. What she is trying to do is offer Joshua a no-fault explanation of his adoption.

"Daddy and me cried too," Joshua's mommy says. "We wanted a baby. But no baby grew inside me. We were very sad."

Joshua has heard this story many times, in response to the same question, probably in the same words. Why, then, when it gets to his own birth, does he show no trace of pleasure? Because he cannot yet accept a no-fault explanation. Beneath any explanation, no matter how fair and feeling, lies the fact that his mother of birth gave him up to someone else. How can he understand that a teen-ager, who looks like a grown woman to him, is still a girl? He cannot see a difference. How can he understand about earning a living? All grown-ups have money. Concrete as his mother has tried to keep the reasons, Joshua knows too little about the obligations of parenting to believe they were the cause of his rejection. Besides, to a child's mind, everything has to be somebody's fault.

Joshua can cast blame in three directions, none correct and none very helpful to him. He can blame his biological mother, his adoptive mother, or himself. He probably does all three, fantasizing in any direction that would lead him to, if not a happy beginning, at least one that makes sense to him. The sense of what his mother tells him now, however wise, however true and convincing to us, eludes him.

"And that was the problem. They could have a baby. But they couldn't take care of one. We could take care of a baby. But we couldn't have one. Your other mother and father decided to let their baby be adopted. We decided to adopt a baby."

"Then I was born!" says Joshua.

These are the ways in which Joshua might manufacture his own sense as his mother continues the story.

His biological mother might not have wanted him because he was a bad boy. Later in the day, an aunt will remark that he was a troublesome baby. His biological mother might not have wanted him because he injured her at birth. Most children have heard some scrap of information about the pain or bleeding of childbirth. His biological mother might not have wanted him because she was a bad person. Some adults still prefer to think that. Or his biological mother did want him, but his adoptive parents stole him away. They're the bad ones.

None of these explanations suits the truth, but any and all of them suit Joshua's four-year-old view of life. He didn't arrive at this view because he was adopted, but because he is a child. To a child's mind, people are either good or bad. Good people do only good things—which does not include giving babies away. Bad people do only bad things—which includes kidnapping. And bad children? They are punished—or banished.

"Then you were born. Our telephone rang. 'We have a baby boy for you,' the doctor said."

The simplicity—we used to call it innocence—of children both startles and amuses us. We are startled to hear the severity of their moral outlook: they will threaten a naughty doll with beheading, and think that a fine and rightful punishment. We are amused at their moral corruption: They will deny snitching a cookie with the crumbs still on their lips. It is a transparent ploy to be sure, but what must be understood is that at two or three it is not you the child is trying to deceive, but himself. Trapped with his own rigid ideas of good and bad, he is in a tight fix about where to put his own badness. Not inside himself—a thought as horrifying as that of a skeleton inside his own smooth skin. So he performs a feat of magic: he splits himself. All the good can stay inside him—the beginnings of a healthy and positive self-image. But for a while, all the bad thoughts, wishes, and actions are cast out like so many devils to show up in dolls and pets, imaginary friends or others who are convenient at the moment.

Such a feat of magic can be performed on parents as well. If you occasionally feel you have acted like a witch or an ogre, a two-year-old would agree. But he would go one step further. You didn't just act like one, you were one. It is as difficult for a child to love a mother who has a witch inside her as it is to love himself with a bad child inside him. So, in the dreams, play, and fantasies of earliest childhood there are not two but four parents: a good mother and a witch, a good father and an ogre.

"You came to us on Thanksgiving day. All the family came too. Your aunts. Your uncles. Your cousins."

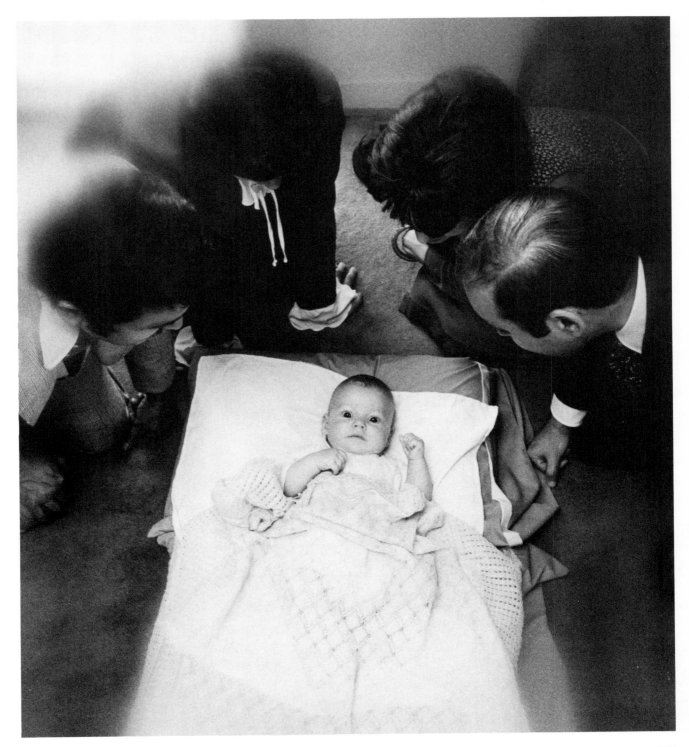

Children routinely give up this rather desperate magic as they grow because their parents support a different view of reality. Maybe you remember a time you were enraged at your child, noticed he was frightened, and wrapped your arms about him in apology. You, the witch, are at the same time a good mommy. Maybe you remember saying something like "You may hate me, but you can't bite me." With your permission, your child can have bad feelings, at the same time that you protect him from harmful actions. Or, "You broke my favorite lamp! I know you were only trying to help." Your child can do a bad thing, with good intentions.

Little by little, children take their parents' moderation into themselves. At first, it may be out loud, as when a child mimics a just parental voice to effect a compromise between good and bad dolls or puppets. Finally, silently, the voice of moderation permanently integrates all the strengths and failings, the generous thoughts and unkind wishes, into a harmony that we call personality.

But this baby, Joshua Thanksgiving, will have a harder time of it.

"They said we should name you Joshua Thanksgiving, because you were a gift from your parents to us."

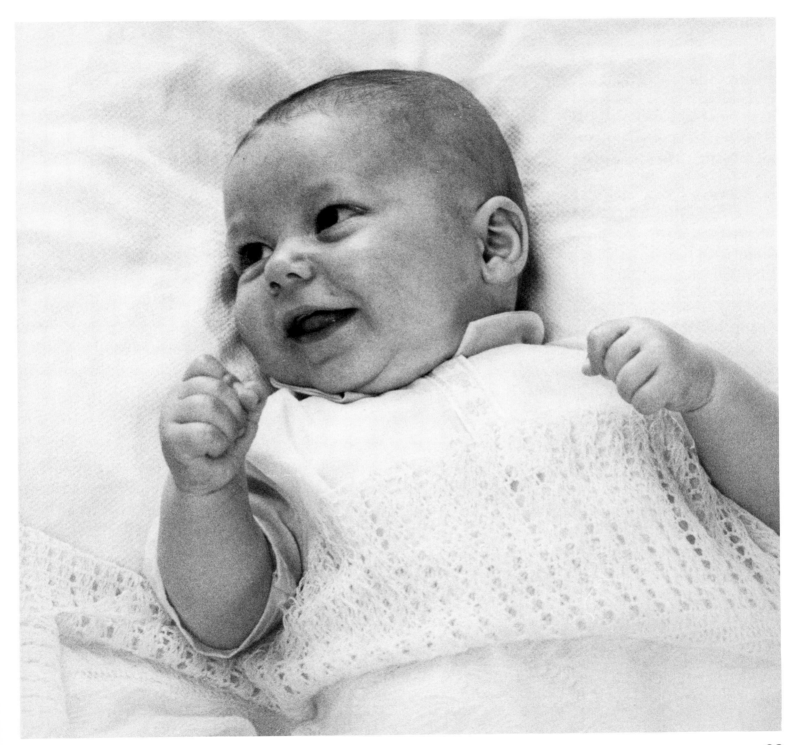

Adopted children do not face different issues than natural children. They face different obstacles. When they, like all children, fear their mother will not come home from an evening out or will never come back to pick them up at school, the fact of an original abandonment is an obstacle to trust. When they are scolded or punished, their fear of rejection has some basis in fact. When they themselves are overwhelmed with anger, the indisputable unfairness that marked their birth stands in the way of reparation. And when both fear and anger invent an imaginary friend or nightmare witch, that inviolate fantasy of an ideal mother is a barrier to integration.

Adoptive parents have to do what every parent has to do, only more so. For the child who fears abandonment, more assurances, more reliability and no threats that he will ever be left behind for bad behavior. For the child who is angry, more acceptance of his reasons and more protection from acting upon them. And for the child who enacts his ideas of good and bad in frightening dreams and patent denials, more insistence that hugging and scolding, help with the housework and strewn playthings, back talk and sweet talk all fit together into the same person.

And more patience. It takes much, much longer for an adopted child to sort out the fantasies from the facts of his life. He cannot get away from the paradox: His "real" mother is a fact that can only be fantasized. There at the core of things is a knot that cannot be untangled. No story could be good enough for Joshua.

That's a good story. But not good enough for Joshua.

In his thoughts and in his actions, Joshua will spend many years probing for the substance of his identity. He will test out what he is and what he is not allowed to do by the usual childhood vocabulary of whining, shouting, nagging, throwing tantrums and poking fingers in the jelly. The limits that his parents set for him, like the moderation they express, will become a part of him. We would not know ourselves without our conscience.

And the fact that Joshua's family has cranberry jelly instead of cranberry sauce, homemade instead of canned, served in slices instead of whole— and always on the same glass plate—these little things will also become a part of him.

Joshua may not look like his parents and his relatives, perhaps his personality will surprise them too, but out of these rich and reliable materials—that snapshot of his first day home, that sliced red jelly on the glass plate, these hanging pots and many cousins and noisy dinners— he will shape his identity. As Joshua grows up in this family, their ways will enter him. He would not know himself without them.

Maybe his real mother would let him stick his fingers in the cranberry jelly.

Each family has to come to know their child too. We do not ever know a child when he is born. Whether he is delivered of us or to us, he is a stranger. Just as Joshua can fantasize an ideal parent, so might his family have fantasized an ideal child. We all do that before the stranger comes. Then we find out. The materials from which a child shapes himself, the ways we believe we can shape him, are only part of the story.

Each baby comes into the world with so prevailing a nature of his own that he shapes us. We thought we could cuddle for hours, but this baby says no. We knew he wouldn't suck his thumb, but he does. We were sure he would be peaceful, but he isn't. So we mother him and father him differently than we envisioned to suit the person he already is.

An adoptive family may find this fact of life particularly difficult. They may fear their child will be too different, foreign from themselves. They would feel their situation to be less unique, perhaps, if they talked with other parents about their natural children. Try it. You are sure to discover a monotone among musicians, a bookworm among baseball fans, a bug lover among bug haters. Only the odds are different.

It is for every parent to nourish where nourishment is needed, no matter how surprising the personality that unfolds.

Though he may certainly object to Joshua pushing the spoon away so rudely, his father would be wise to accept this asparagus hater among asparagus lovers. There are other things to eat.

Maybe his real father wouldn't make him eat asparagus.

Maybe in that family it would be okay to spill milk.

This reasonable mommy who scolds a little but wipes the mess and refills the glass doesn't fit very well with the idea of a wicked stepmother. Of course, it isn't possible to do the right thing every time. When the relatives accuse Joshua of being troublesome, they are making a mistake that most of us make when we are pushed to such irritation. We generalize and categorize. Our wives are sloppy, our children selfish, and our husbands never take us out to dinner.

Criticism is better kept to specifics. That Joshua spoiled the perfect slices of cranberry jelly today is an issue. That does not mean he is "always" into everything. Whether he ate well or poorly as a baby has nothing to do with a dislike of asparagus. And though he has been rude at dinner, it is unfair to classify his very nature as "troublesome."

Criticisms which condemn a child's nature rather than a specific behavior cannot help but complicate efforts to make peace between the good and bad. Concerned as he has been all day with his place in the family, wondering whether his biological parents might have been nicer, worrying about his own role in his rejection, these remarks are fuel for an explosion.

Aunt Jane says he certainly was a troublesome baby. He never did eat well.

Uncle Henry says he certainly is a troublesome boy. Always into everything.

Left out by his cousins, unconvinced by his mother, scolded by his father, and now criticized by his aunts and uncles, the rage that has been building all day explodes. These people are not his "real" relatives. This is not his "real" mother and father. Joshua enacts his own rejection.

The extent of rage in adopted children is not hard to understand, but we rebel at accepting it. We are the good guys who have come to the rescue, who do our best and love wholeheartedly. Why should we be paid in anger? Yet that has to be. Joshua's fury is in him, as much as his kisses are. His reasons are real. He was given away, separated forever from that other mother, from her family of aunts and uncles, cousins and grandparents; from her stories and snapshots, her childhood and neighborhood; from her face, arms, songs and ways in which he might have seen himself reflected. We cannot love half a child. So we have to say, to Joshua and to all adopted children, how awful. How unfair. How angry a thing this is, to be adopted.

"You're not my real mommy and daddy," yells Joshua.

But that's the way it is. Joshua is stuck with a lifelong accident: a group of people who, by a stranger's pain and a woman's desire, by many people's intelligent efforts and the crazy swing of chance, became his family.

Yet who does get to choose their parents? When things aren't going well, it must cross the mind of every child that perhaps he could have done better, could have landed in a nicer, richer family than these mean people who do not give him all he asks for or dote on all he does. Similar thoughts can cross the minds of parents too. The accident of conception could have handed out fewer whines and higher grades, or dropped a dimple in the right place.

Once in a while it might be of benefit in any family to tell the bare truth: We may not like each other all the time, but we are stuck with one another. We are a family. Joshua's mother and father may not be "real" in Joshua's sense, but they are really his.

"You're not our real child either," Daddy yells back.

What Joshua's father tells him is the kernel of what adopted children must accept. They can't accept it at three or six or even at ten. Perhaps they can't settle for it until they come to terms with their parents' faults—and their own—when they are past their teen-age years and approaching adulthood. And maybe they can't live comfortably with our best efforts to solve an insoluble problem until they are all the way grown up and can see that most of us must live without final answers to our most troubling questions.

Right now Joshua can only begin. With all his fears and fantasies, his consuming wishes and shattering angers, there is one clear reality. Who we get as parents and who we get as children is never, whether the relationship is natural or adoptive, under our control. That, for parent and child alike, is the surprise. But the human bond of obligation, acceptance and love grows anyway. That is the gift.

"But you're the only child we have. People don't choose the gifts they get. They are surprises."

"And we have always loved surprises."